# CHRISTMAS EVE

## EASY PIANO SOLO

7777 W. BLUEMOUND RD. P.O. BOX 13819 MILWAUKEE, WI 53213

Visit Hal Leonard Online at
**www.halleonard.com**

ISBN 978-1-4234-4176-2

# CHRISTMAS EVE

◆

## CONTENTS

## CHRISTMAS EVE

Winter is the time when Mother Earth takes a breath inward, and I believe it very natural for us to pause and do the same – to allow ourselves time for introspection amidst all the celebration and activity of the holidays. The music of CHRISTMAS EVE was created during such a time in my own life.

Though the arrangements for some of these carols and the idea for the album began in the Winter of 1990, most of the work and all of the recording occurred at home during an "extended Christmas respite" that followed a very rigorous touring schedule during most of 1993.

As the work progressed and each carol developed from fragments and wisps to finished works, I imagined that an Angel, a Guardian Angel of sorts, existed for each of the songs. These Angels seemed to guide my hand and heart throughout the process. They also resulted in the seven Angel Improvisations threaded between the carols. Musical inward breaths.

If the music encourages your own quiet introspections, that was my hope and intention. This mood is surely the very essence of the spirit of the holiday. But if you do take that inward breath, don't be surprised if you feel a light brush of Angel wings and hear the softest of whispers…

Wishing you peace and God's blessings,

*David Lanz*

*"Above the deep and dreamless sleep, the silent stars go by."*

# ANGEL OF COMFORT

Composed by
DAVID LANZ

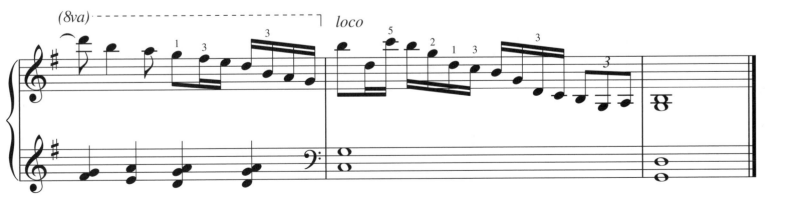

# ANGELS WE HAVE HEARD ON HIGH

Arranged by
DAVID LANZ

**Flowing**

*With pedal*

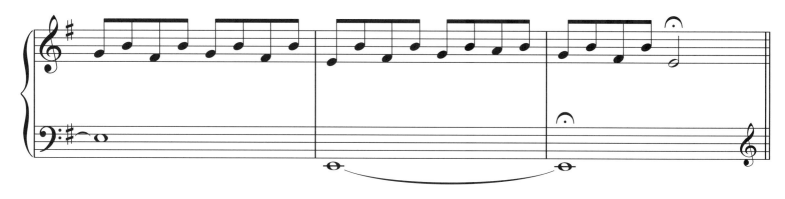

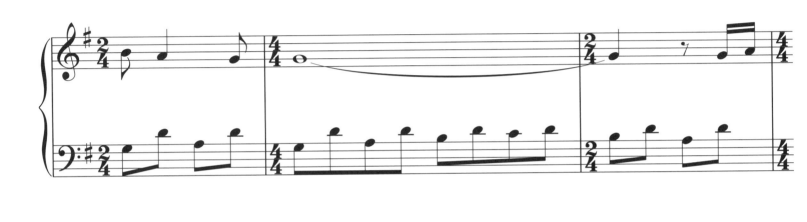

*Both hands 8vb (2nd time)*

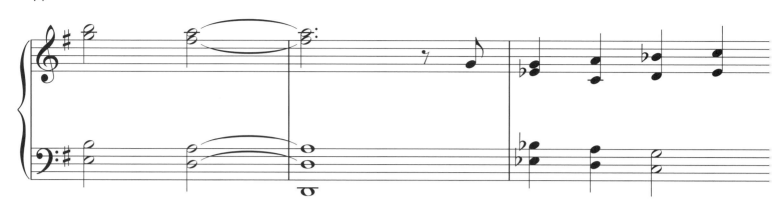

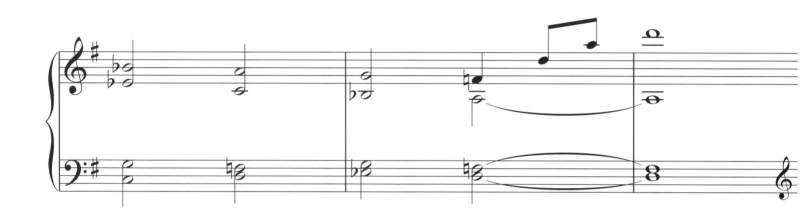

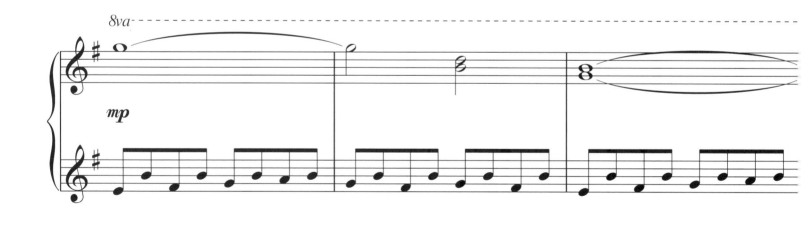

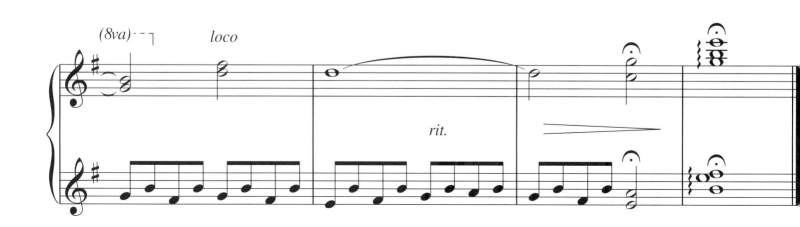

# GOD REST YE MERRY, GENTLEMEN

Arranged by
DAVID LANZ

**With motion**

*With pedal*

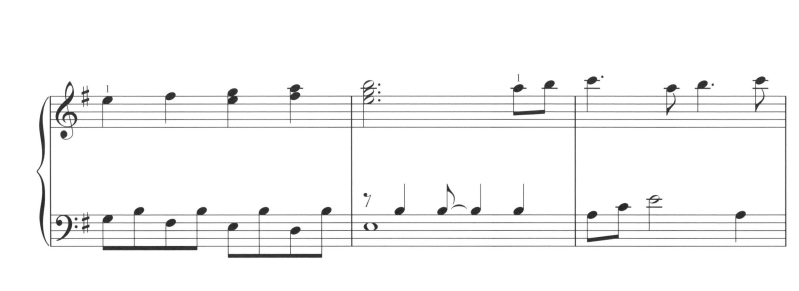

**To Coda** $\oplus$

**D.S. al Coda**

**CODA**

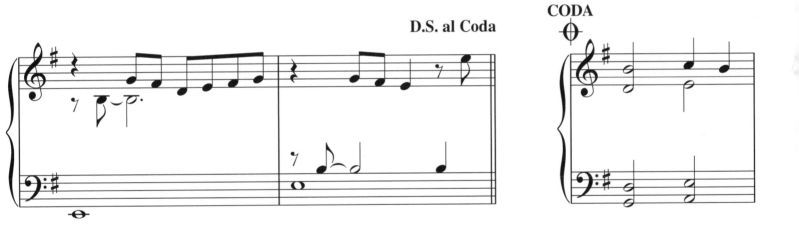

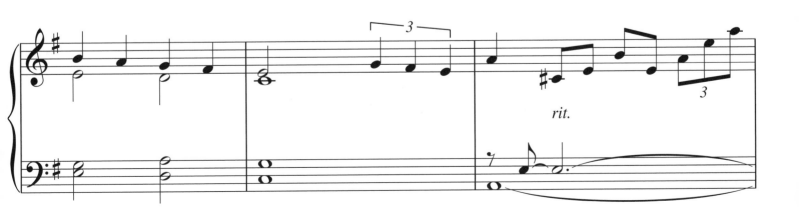

*rit.*

**Slower**

# ANGEL OF JOY

Composed by
DAVID LANZ

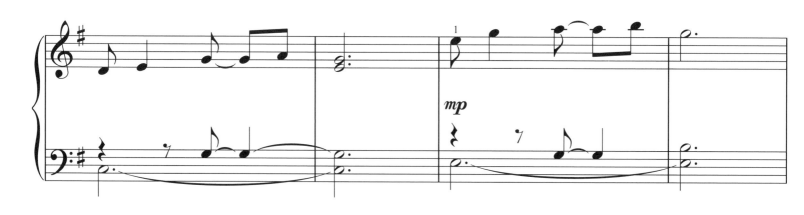

# O COME, ALL YE FAITHFUL

Arranged by
DAVID LANZ

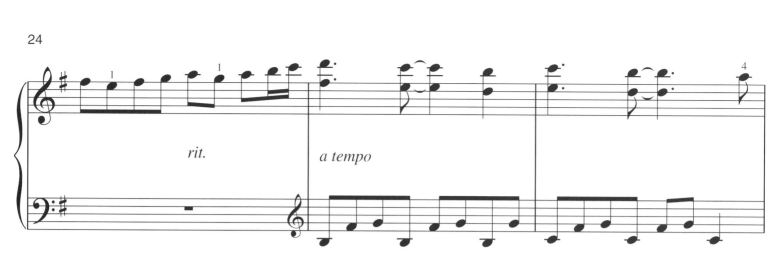

rit.                a tempo

rit.

a tempo

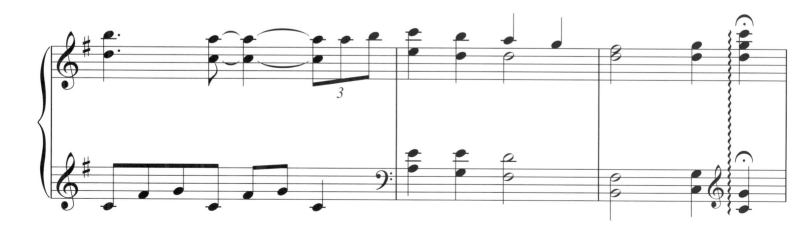

# THE ANGEL KING

Composed by
DAVID LANZ

# THE FIRST NOËL/
# CHRISTMAS EVE WALTZ

Composed and Arranged by
DAVID LANZ

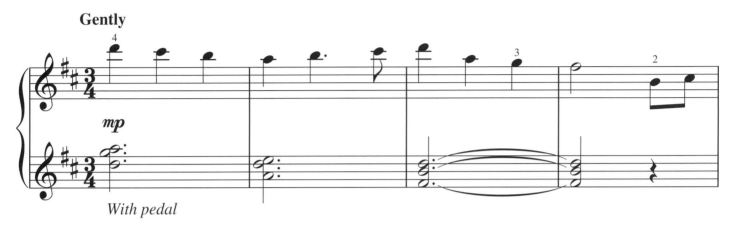

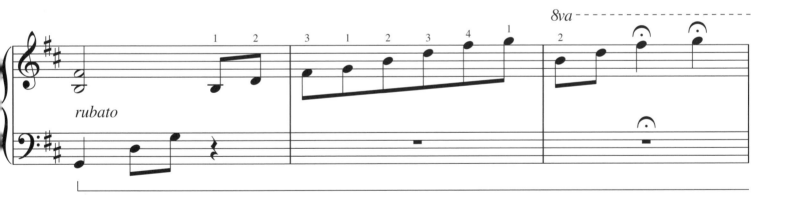

**To Coda** ⊕

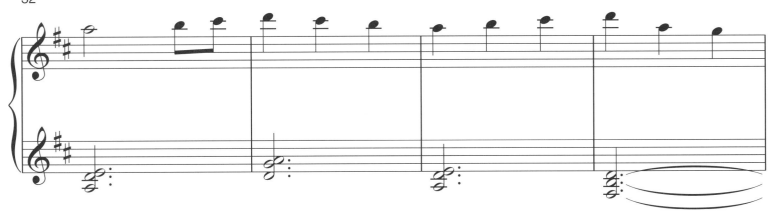

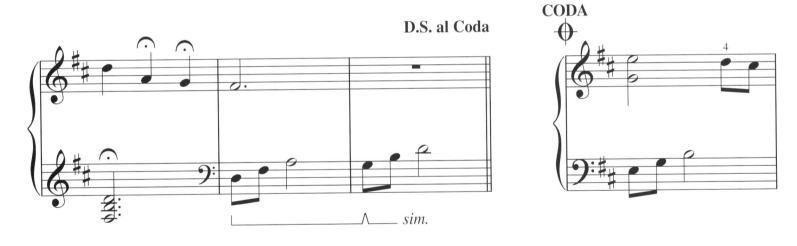

**D.S. al Coda**

**CODA**

# JOY TO THE WORLD

Arranged by
DAVID LANZ

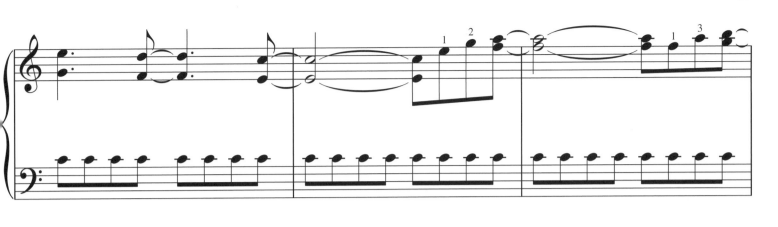

**To Coda**

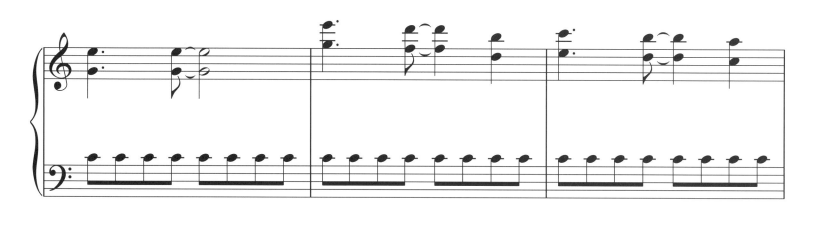

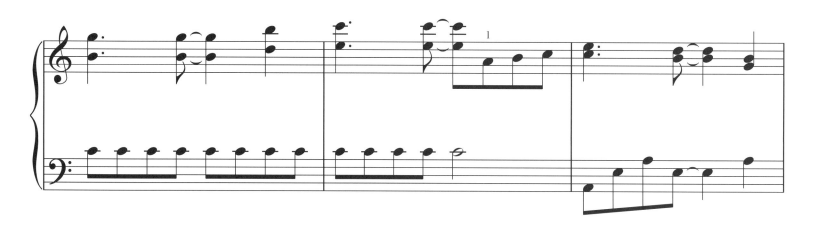

# O LITTLE TOWN OF BETHLEHEM

Arranged by
DAVID LANZ

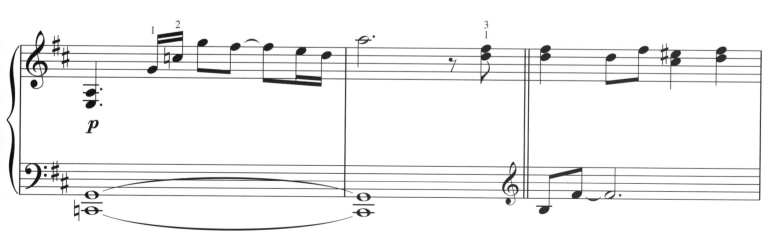

# ANGEL OF HOPE

Composed by
DAVID LANZ

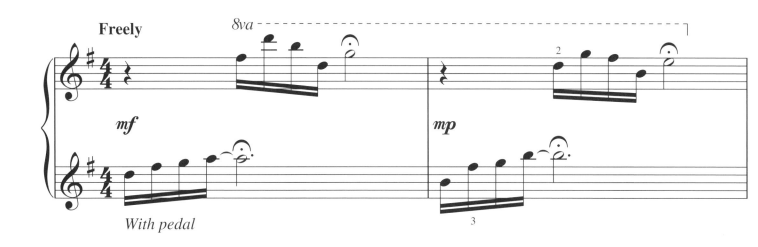

Gently, in tempo

rit.

a tempo

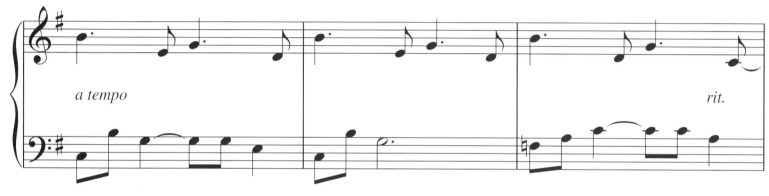

# O COME, O COME, EMMANUEL

Arranged by
DAVID LANZ

# A BRUSH OF WINGS

Composed by
DAVID LANZ

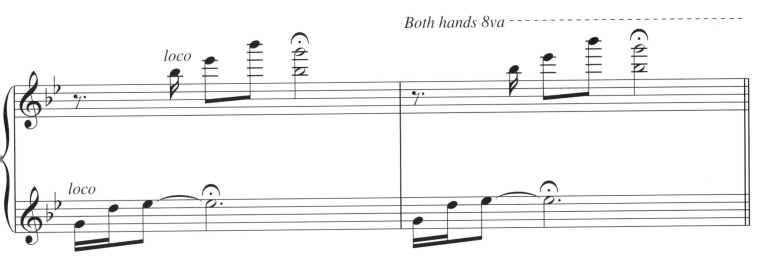

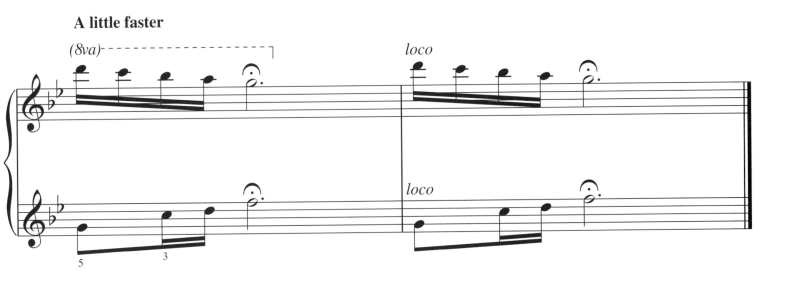

# WHAT CHILD IS THIS

Arranged by
DAVID LANZ

**Gently**

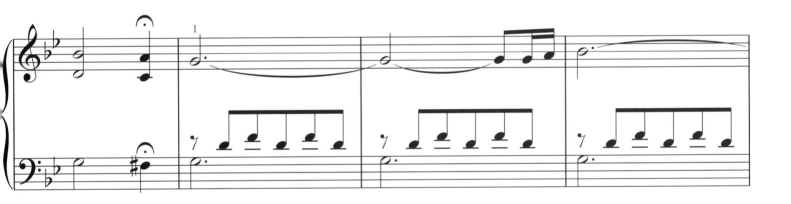

# AN ANGEL AT MIDNIGHT

Composed by
DAVID LANZ

# "I SAW THE PATH OF THE ANGELS"

Composed by
DAVID LANZ

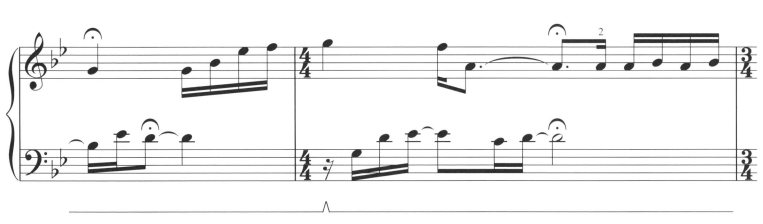

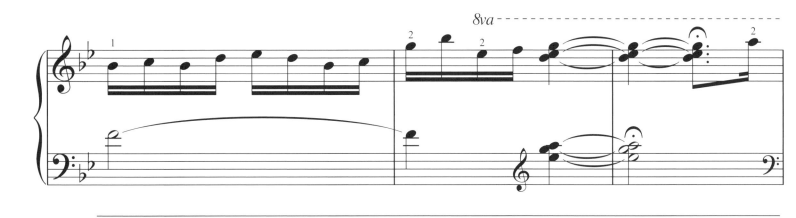

# SILENT NIGHT

Arranged by
DAVID LANZ

slower

a tempo

70

# O HOLY NIGHT

Arranged by
DAVID LANZ

**Slightly faster**

**A little faster**

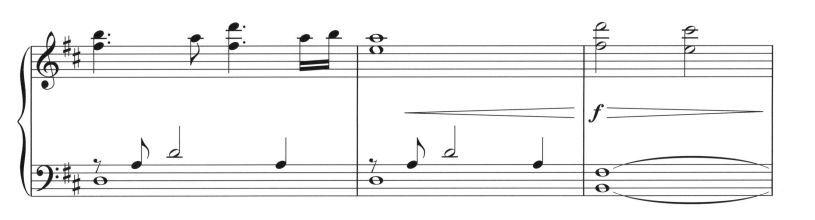

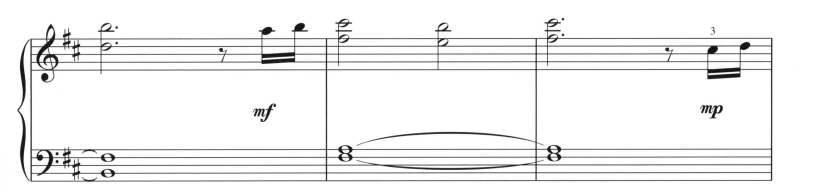